The Language of Animals

the
LANGUAGE
of ANIMALS
by Millicent E. Selsam

Illustrated by Kathleen Elgin

WILLIAM MORROW & CO., NEW YORK 1962

Library of Congress Catalog Card Number 62-7714

The author wishes to thank
Dr. William N. Tavolga
of the American Museum of Natural History
for checking the manuscript of this book.

CONTENTS

CHAPTER 1

The Animal's Point of View

Animals do not have a language like ours. They do not talk to each other in words and sentences. In fact, most animals cannot say a single word. But we only have to watch them to see that they communicate with each other by signals of some kind.

A school of minnows comes close to shore, and as we approach their silvery bodies flash in unison. The whole school goes off together in another direction. Flocks of starlings come in to roost on a winter evening and shift and turn and dive together with the greatest precision. The monkeys in a zoo, the dogs on a street, the chickens in a barnyard, the minnows, the starlings, and most other animals have ways of communicating with one another.

But how can we find out about their secret worlds? How can we be sure of what an animal sees, hears, tastes, or smells?

It is easy enough to imagine that their worlds are just like ours. We find it natural to think that they see what we see, hear what we hear, and smell the same odors we do. But if you think this way, you are bound to make mistakes.

Once, as a young teacher-in-training, I was asked to get down on the floor and sing to a turtle. My superior was sure that turtles loved music. I asked her if she thought they preferred classical or jazz. "Classical," she said. And so I got as close as I could to the turtle and sang a theme from a Beethoven symphony. The turtle wagged his head back and forth, "almost in time to the music," my boss said. But somebody should have told us that it could not possibly hear anything, since a turtle is deaf.

A snake is deaf too. But you can read stories and see pictures of snake charmers in Indian bazaars playing music to charm their deadly poisonous cobra snakes. If you watch such a performance, it looks as though the snake is listening and responding to the music. But a scientist became interested in this and did some tests. He blindfolded the cobra. Then he beat on tin cans and blew bugles near the cobra. There was no reaction. When the blindfolds were removed, the experimenter waved his arms around, and the cobra immediately raised its head and spread its hood. And so we found out that snakes are charmed not by the sound of music, but by the movements the snake charmer makes as he plays.

Imagine yourself sitting in a living room with a dog beside you, a bird in a cage, and a fish swimming in an aquarium. Each is in its own world. The dog can't see colors and in general can't see as well as we do. But he can smell the faintest odors and hear much higher sounds than we can. The bird has keen eyes but hardly any sense of smell. The fish is nearsighted in its watery world, but has taste organs in its skin that make it sensitive to chemicals or dissolved food in the water. If we want to find out how fish communicate with fish, or dogs with dogs, we must find out what their particular worlds are like. We must look at animals from the animal's point of view.

There are two ways to go about investigating this question. One way is by observing animals in the environment where they are living their natural lives. Scientists have spent years in remote places doing just this. They have watched colonies of gulls on lonely islands. They have followed herds of deer on mountain slopes. They have spent years in tropical jungles watching the daily doings of clans of monkeys. As they observe these animals, they may think of explanations for their behavior, and then test these ideas out by experiment. For example, they may hear gulls making certain sounds when they find food. Are these sounds a call to other gulls? Scientists can test this by recording this food-finding call and then broadcasting it through a loud-speaker. If the gulls gather then, they will have evidence that this particular sound attracts other gulls to new-found food.

While many observations and experiments are made "in the field" with wild animals, others are done in zoos or aquariums or laboratories with captive animals. Every experiment sets out to answer a question. If something in the surroundings of a group of animals is changed, how will the animals react? And most important, how does their behavior compare with that of a group kept under normal surroundings (*control group*)? Many precautions must be taken to make sure that the animals are reacting only to the sounds or sights the scientist is providing, and not to something else. Even the experimenter himself can get in the way of an experiment with animals.

For many years, scientists had to rely on written descriptions of the sounds of animals. But in the last fifteen years, wonderful advances in electronic machines have made it possible to record animal sounds accurately. Battery-operated tape recorders are carried into the field, turned on, and all the trills, grunts, knocks, and songs of the animal world are perma-

tape recorder

nently recorded on spools of tape. Special instruments turn recorded sounds into pictures. Some sounds may seem the same to our ears, but look very different when recorded on paper in these sound spectrograms. The use of such electronic equipment has put the study of animal sounds on a new level.

Animal communication is a new branch of science. Much of the information reported in this book has only recently been discovered. Some ideas we now think are true may change with further experimental work. But that is the very nature of all science—ever-changing and developing.

CHAPTER 2

Underwater Signals

During World War II, the "silent world" of the sea was found to be quite noisy. In the spring of 1942, the Navy was testing new underwater microphones (hydrophones), which were intended to detect the sound of enemy submarines, in the Chesapeake Bay area. After sunset every evening, the machines picked up a racket of strange sounds. The Navy men heard beeps, groans, crackles, grunts, moans, and other noises through their earphones.

Scientists who were consulted thought that the undersea uproar might be caused by animals. They were right. Soon they were able to prove that the biggest noisemakers were fish.

The Noise Fish Make

One of the loudest noisemakers is the croaker, or drumfish, that moves into the Bay each spring to breed. Schools of these

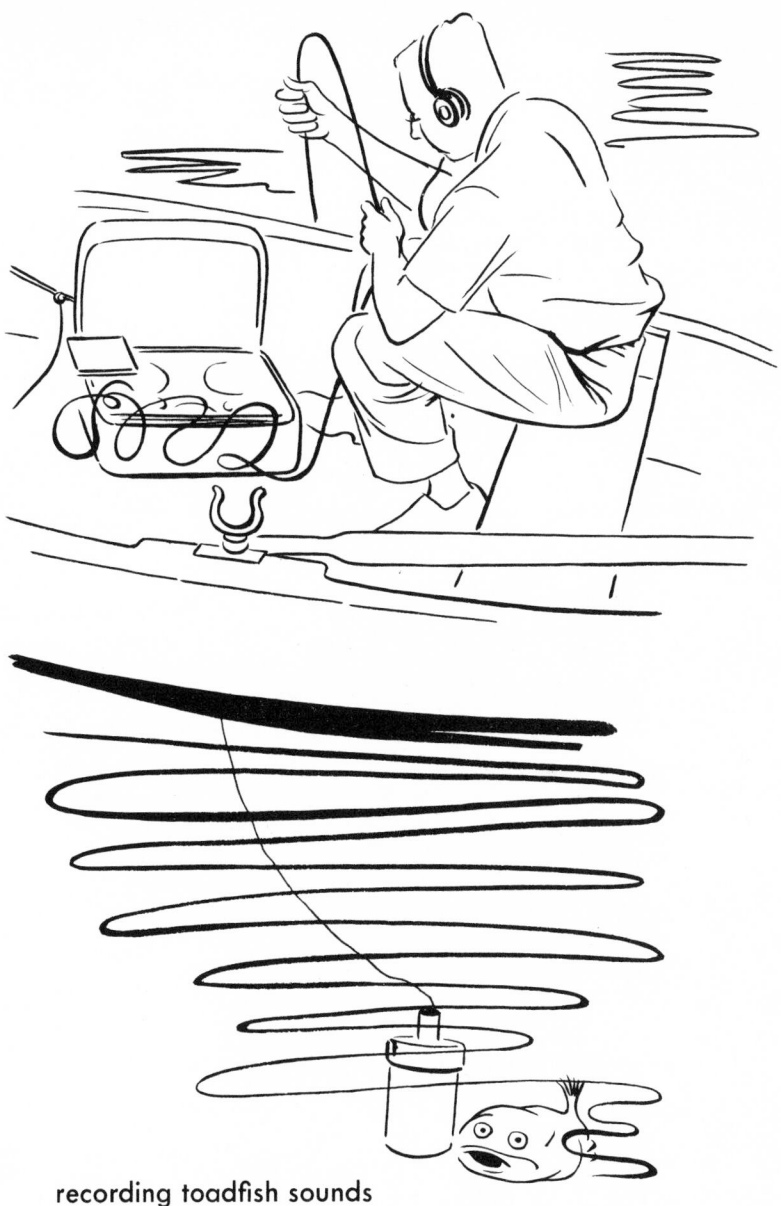

recording toadfish sounds

fish make sounds like the beating of many drums. Sea catfish grunt. When a whole school of them grunt together, they sound like a giant coffee percolator. The toadfish, an ugly sluggish bottom fish, grunts too. But it also gives out a *boop* like a steamboat whistle. Sound in the sea travels four to five times faster than its speed in air, and if you are an underwater skin diver close to a toadfish when he blasts off, it might hurt your ears. The sea robin squawks and cackles like a chicken. Even in the laboratory it keeps up a grunting, cackling noise all the time.

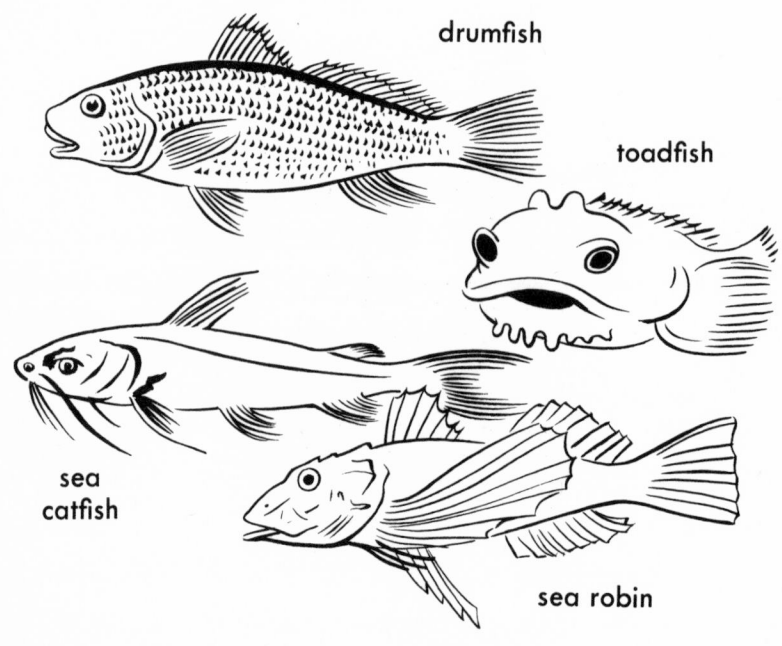

drumfish

toadfish

sea
catfish

sea robin

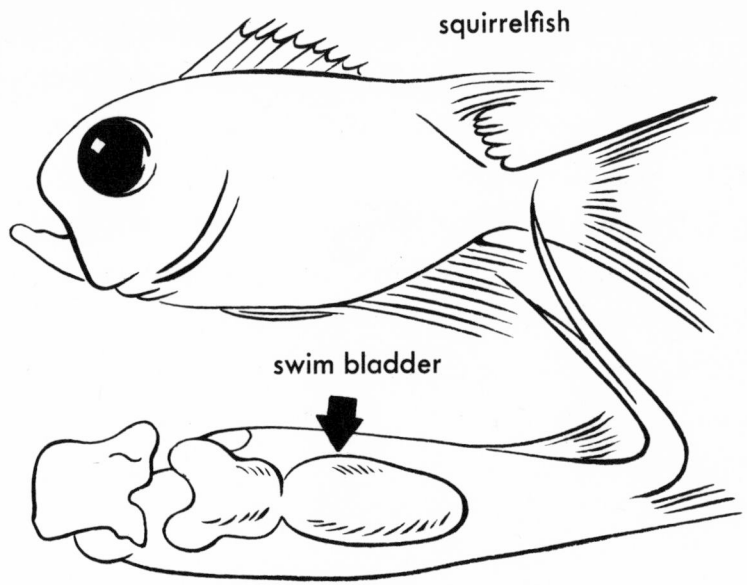

squirrelfish

swim bladder

(as seen from below after dissection)

How do the fish produce these sounds? They do not have vocal cords and lungs like ours, but they have other ways of making noise. Many of them have air or swim bladders inside them that act like internal drums. The swim bladder is a balloonlike sac that lies inside the body of the fish just under the backbone. Special muscles in the walls, or attached to them, contract and make the bladder vibrate with a low-pitched, drumlike sound. But other fish make sounds in other ways. They may grind their teeth, or snap the spines of their fins, or rub bones together to make rasping, scratchy sounds. The puffer grates the upper and lower bones that look like teeth in its beaklike mouth. This produces long bursts of *erk-erks* like the sound of a saw going back and forth through wood. The sea horse makes a sound like the snapping of a finger against a thumb, when it lifts its head from its usual position at right angles to its body and rubs two bony edges of its skeleton together. Teeth in the back of the mouth of the parrot fish grate together and make a scratchy, crackling sound.

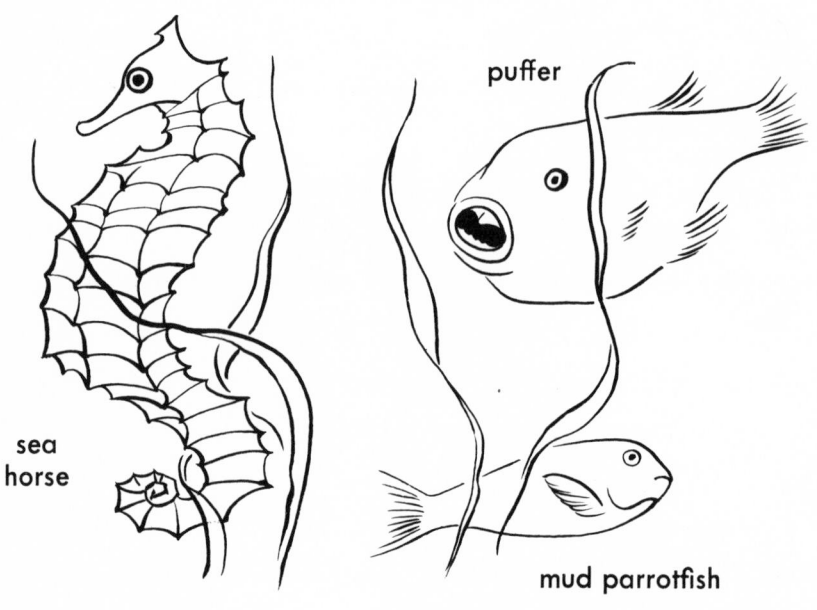

sea
horse

puffer

mud parrotfish

What Fish Hear

The next question is, "Can fish hear the sounds they produce?" Fish have no ears on the outside of their head, and for this reason most people thought fish were deaf. But a few disagreed. Long ago in a monastery in Austria, the monks kept carp in a big pond. A monk rang a bell each time the fish were fed, and the fish swam to their feeding place. It did look as though the fish were responding to the bell. But then a biologist discovered that the fish were really swimming toward the monk because they saw him. They came toward the monk even when he did not ring the bell. Nothing was really proved by this. Perhaps the fish heard and perhaps they did not.

Another scientist actually got into a pool with his fish to watch their reaction when he banged a steel plate very loudly. He could hardly bear the horrible racket, but the fish paid no attention at all. It still looked as though fish could not hear.

Then a group of scientists did some important new experiments. They started from the idea that a sound could become meaningful to a fish if it received its food *only when that sound was made.* They made sure that the fish were not seeing the experimenter and responding to him. Then the fish, which were minnows, were taught to swim forward for their food at the sound of a certain note. If they came forward when higher or lower notes were sounded, they were punished by a blow from a glass rod. By repeating this over and over, the scientists trained the fish to move forward and snap at food only when they heard the feeding note and never at the warning note. Then the interval between these two sounds was reduced. In this way, they found out that these fish could be trained to tell the difference beween two sounds an octave apart.

Later these scientists improved their techniques and were able to show that minnows could hear under water just as well as a human being! Fish have inner ears hidden inside their head. They are just little sacs containing cells sensitive to sound waves. When these are removed from a fish, it cannot hear. So even without outside ears, fish can hear the sounds other fish make.

The Meaning of Fish Sounds

But do these sounds mean anything in the life of a fish? Are there mating calls that help male and female fish come together at the breeding season? Do some fish sounds help to keep off intruders or warn their fellow fish? Do sounds serve to keep groups of fish together in dark, murky waters when sight is impossible? These are the questions to which scientists are just beginning to find answers.

Sea catfish, as we have seen, grunt—and a whole chorus of them sounds like the perking of a "giant coffee percolator." During the day these sounds are not heard. But when darkness falls, groups of catfish can easily be located with listening gear. These sounds are heard outside of the usual breeding season, and so scientists have concluded that they probably help keep the fish together at night when the fish cannot see. The sounds of eels, croakers, and sea robins may also serve the same purpose. These fish either live in muddy, dark waters, or are active mostly at night.

Sound plays an important role in the life of the goby. Only the male goby fish makes sounds. They are low-pitched thumps, and are made only while courting the female. If a male goby fish in a glass flask is put into a tank containing female gobies, nothing much happens. But if a microphone in the tank is turned on and the male's thump sound is played through it, so that the female fish can both see the male and hear the thumping sound, there is a definite reaction. The females approach the male goby, enclosed in the flask, and scramble over the glass and the microphone near it. Male gobies will move toward the male thumping sound too. So here we have clear evidence that sound helps males and females meet when egg-laying (spawning) time comes.

The toadfish makes two sounds—the *boop* like a steam

gobies

whistle and a short grunt. In a tank in a laboratory the toad-fish answers every prod or push with a grunt. This sound may warn enemies away. The *boop* sound may keep other fish away from its territory, or it may have something to do with mating during the spawning season. But we still do not know because toadfish will not *boop* when they are kept in aquariums.

And so fish sounds may serve to bring sexes together, to keep other fish away from private territories, to warn off enemies, or to keep fish of one species in contact with each other. But much of this remains to be proved.

Smell Signals

Fish use smell and taste signals as well as sound signals in communicating with each other. Research on these senses of fish has given us some surprising results.

One investigator found that a minnow not only recognizes the smell of its own kind, but can be trained to recognize the odor of fifteen different species of fish! The same experimenter was able to show that a minnow can even tell one member of its group from another. This sharp sense of smell gives the fish protection against its enemies. If water that passed over a pike enters a tank where minnows are kept, the minnows become motionless and sink to the bottom. This protects them, for pike go after moving prey and will pay no attention to a still object.

Fish that live in schools can also communicate danger signals to each other. When an injured minnow is placed among its school of minnows, there is an immediate alarm reaction. The minnows scatter or seek cover. They are reacting to a chemical substance released by the damaged skin of the wounded fish.

Recently an experiment showed that fish which see other fish react in this way to the substance from damaged skin also react the same way. Two aquariums were placed close together. The fish in one aquarium could see the fish in the other, but no smell or taste communication was possible be-

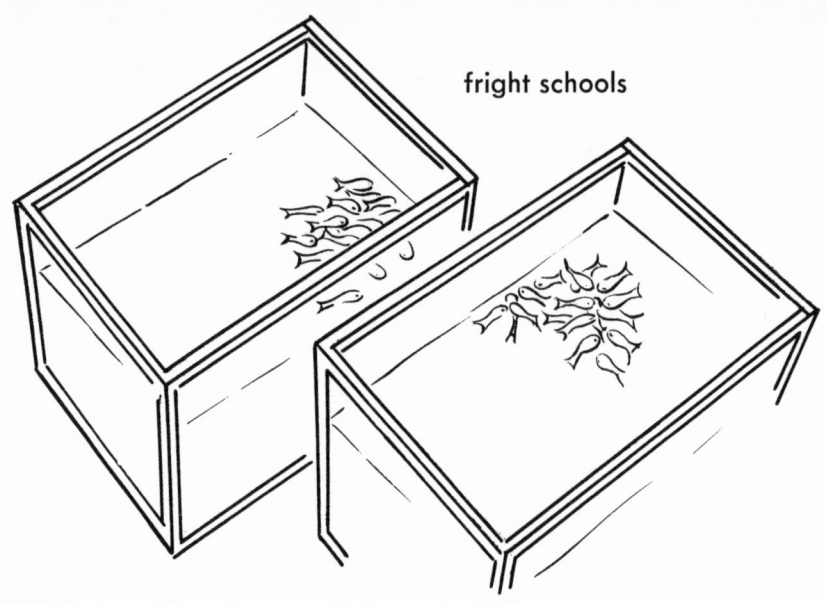

fright schools

cause the fish were in separate aquariums. A drop of juice from damaged skin of the same kind of fish was dropped into one aquarium. The fish in that aquarium showed the fright reaction by huddling together on the bottom in a tight school. The fish in the other tank formed the same kind of huddle on the bottom ten seconds later! Sight alone was enough to communicate the fright reaction.

Sight Signals

Movements of a fish or color changes in its body can operate as signals too. The beautiful tropical jewel fish has iridescent blue spots on the red of its back fin. The female parent jerks her fin up and down making the blue spots flash like jewels. This is a signal to her young. They gather under her and are led to their nest at the bottom of the tank.

jewel fish and young

A lot of sign language goes on in the courtship ceremonies of some fish. In the spring, the male three-spined stickleback digs a pit in the sand of shallow ponds, piles in a heap of water weeds, and then fashions it into a round nest with a

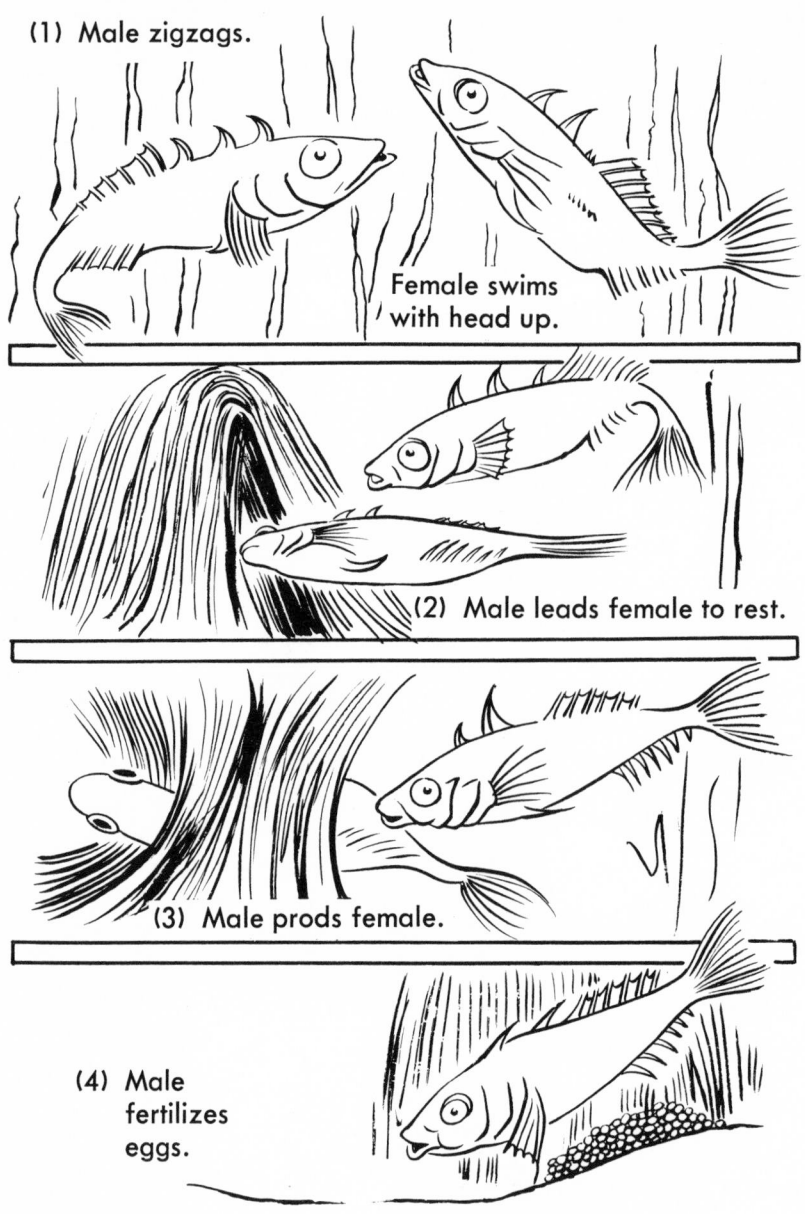

(1) Male zigzags.

Female swims with head up.

(2) Male leads female to rest.

(3) Male prods female.

(4) Male fertilizes eggs.

tunnel through the middle. When the nest is finished, he swims around near it, and his belly turns bright red. The red belly becomes a signal to the female stickleback. When she comes near, the male does a zigzag dance. The dance makes the female swim toward the male with her head up. This is the signal for the male to lead her to the nest. He pushes his snout into the entrance, turns on his side, and raises his spines. The female responds by entering the nest. The male then prods her tail and she lays her eggs. After she leaves, the male enters and fertilizes the eggs. Throughout this whole ceremony, the proper signals must be given in the right order. Otherwise, the courtship breaks off. Without these signals between male and female, new generations of sticklebacks would never be produced.

Many of us at one time or another have seen schools of fish move together in perfect ranks keeping a definite distance between each other. As we watch, they swerve to the right or the left, or suddenly turn completely around, the whole school moving as one. Experiments with mackerel at the New York Aquarium showed that even when only two mackerel see each other, they come together until there is a small but definite distance between them. How do fish keep together this way? And what signals are used?

Blind fish do not school. Covering the eyes of the fish who

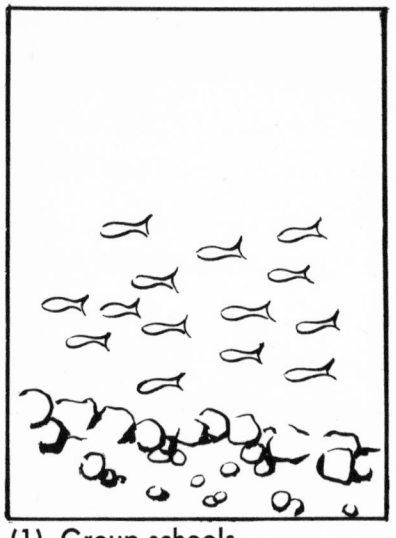

(1) Group schools
under light.

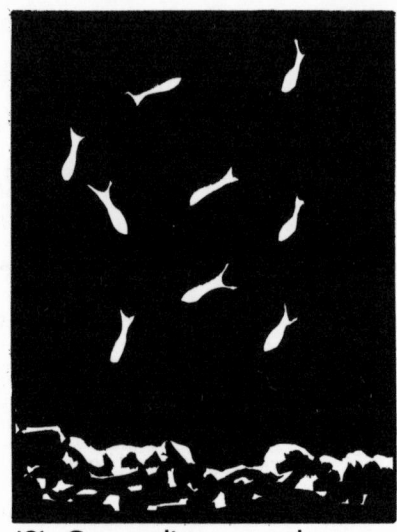

(2) Group disperses when
light is turned off.

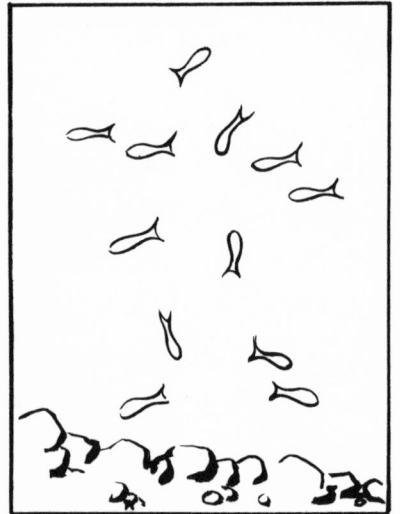

(3) Grouping begins when
light is put on again.

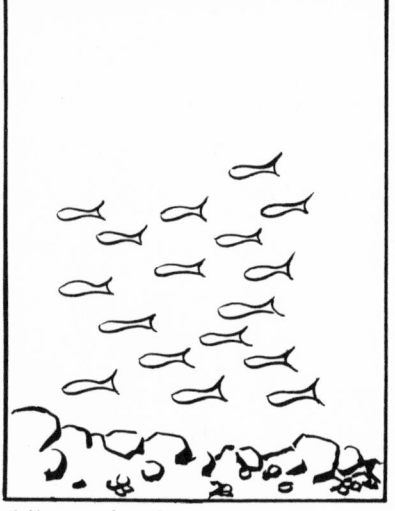

(4) reschooling
completed

school prevents schooling. If a mirror is put into the tank, fish try to school with their own images. Sight is the important stimulus.

Schools of fish usually disperse in darkness. If a light is turned on over such a tank of fish, the fish arrange themselves in a tight school within five minutes. But there are exceptions to every rule. Some fish school at night. Sight cannot be a factor here. Then what keeps these fish together? It could be sound, as we have seen. It could be smell, or possibly a re-

mother porpoise and her baby

sponse to the water currents set up by the fish swimming nearby. We still do not know.

Porpoises

Other animals of the sea beside fish can communicate with each other. Porpoises (often called dolphins) exchange whistles and clicks. In one marine laboratory, 802 whistles were heard in 10½ minutes when a mother porpoise discovered her baby was lost. The porpoise has a double-whistle distress signal to which other porpoises respond. They become silent, search for the source of the signal, and push the distressed porpoise to the surface of the water. Then they exchange whistles with it. With further experiments, scientists hope to find out what the different kinds of whistles and clicks mean in the life of these animals.

Many puzzles about underwater communication signals remain to be solved.

CHAPTER 3

Frog, Snake, and Alligator Language

Frogs and toads around lakes and ponds fill the warm summer nights with their voices. Some are croaking, some are trilling in high, thin tones, and others are bellowing in low notes. "Kerrrooaaak," "peep peep," "jug o' rum," "grunk"— each is calling in its own special way.

If you could see the frog or toad while it is calling, you would notice a sac of skin like a balloon of bubble gum, vibrating under the chin. It is amplifying the sound made as the frog or toad, with its mouth closed, draws air back and forth from its lungs to its mouth over its vocal cords.

Most of the calling is done by males, and it has always been thought that these calls attracted females to the pond and that mating then took place. This was hard to prove, though, until new electronic equipment made it possible to record these sounds and use them in experiments.

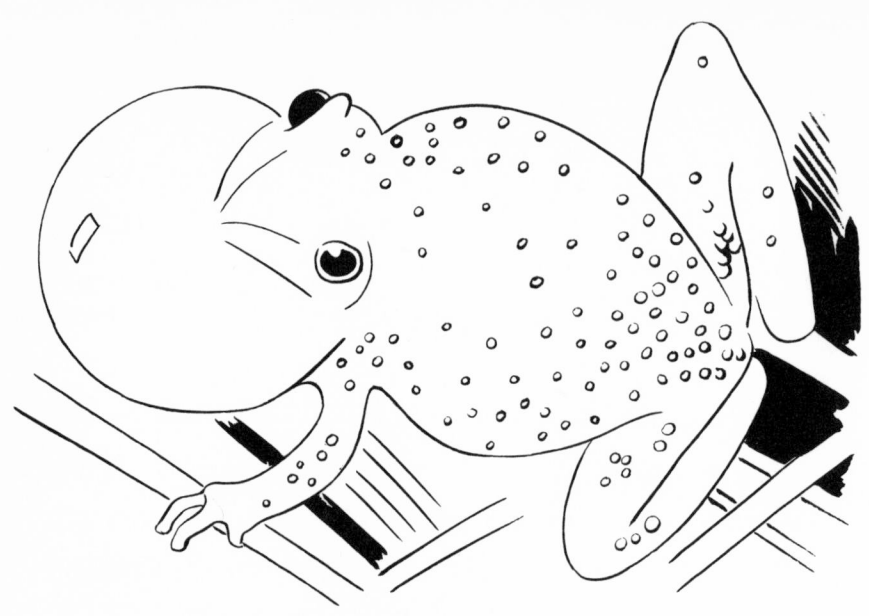

spring peeper calling

In one such experiment, male and female toads were released at night on a paved terrace while a loud-speaker played recordings of a male chorus of the same toads. When the speaker played, the majority of both male and female frogs moved toward it and lined up in a semicircle about seven feet away. A control group was then set free on the same terrace while no sound issued from the loud-speaker. The toads in this group went in all directions.

Another experiment showed that female frogs would move toward calling males even when they were hidden in cloth bags. They also moved toward a microphone playing the male

toads attracted by loud-speaker

call. So we have evidence that male toads and frogs do attract females to the ponds where they are calling. When males are attracted too, they increase the number of male frogs in the pond and swell the chorus that brings females.

Male frogs and toads clasp the females when they get close enough, and hold on till both eggs and sperm are expelled into the water at the same time. As the eggs come out, the sperm fertilize them. How does the male frog tell a female from a male? There may be ways we don't know about—but we do know that if a male happens to be clasped by another male, he croaks and struggles until he is set free. A female re-

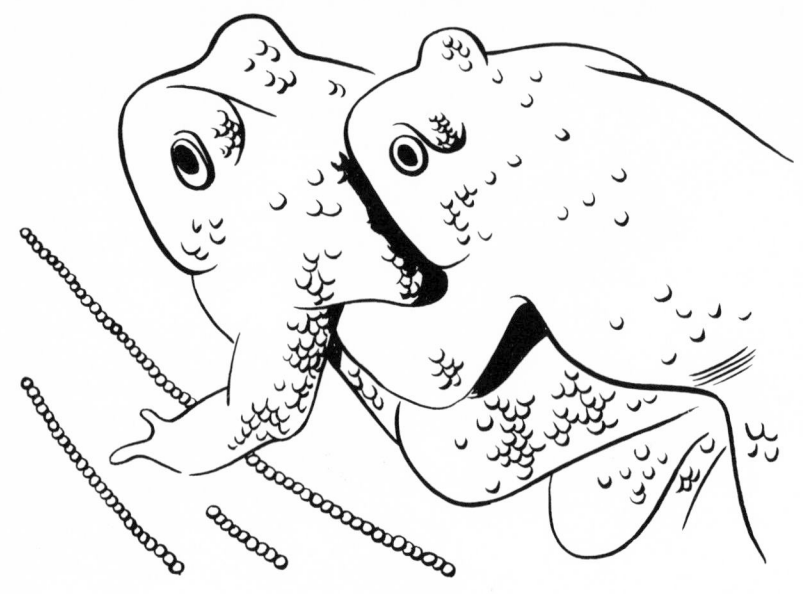

male frog clasping female

mains silent and is held onto until she releases the eggs.

Many different frogs may be calling from a single pond at the same time. Can the female tell her particular kind of frog from any other? A recent experiment seems to prove that she can. The females of a certain kind of frog were released between two microphones. One played the call of their own species. The other microphone played the mating call of a close relative. The females moved toward the call of their own species. There may be sight and smell signals involved here too, but these remain to be discovered.

Although most frog and toad calls have to do with mating, other calls can be heard at times. When frogs are seized by snakes, raccoons, or other animals, they scream. These distress calls probably do not help the poor trapped frog, but they may help other frogs escape. Frogs also have a warning sound they make when disturbed. They chirp or grunt as they dive into the water. The sound of the splash added to the grunt alerts the other frogs. One scientist reported that he couldn't get near frogs in a pond after one jumped in this way.

Snake Language

The snake that catches the frog wouldn't be disturbed by the frog's scream, for snakes cannot hear. Yet you can always read stories like this one that appeared in a well-known magazine. A man was playing a violin on the shore of a lake. Snake after snake crawled out of the woods and came toward him. When he played, one snake vibrated to the music, and as he changed tempo, the snake changed its vibration. If the violinist moved, the snake followed him around. When he stood still, the snake came within six feet of him, curled up, raised its head, and sat there like a statue. The violinist was certain that the snake was responding to his music, and indeed it did seem to be. But a scientist who read this story pointed out that the snake might have been attracted to the movements the man made while playing the violin. The violinist could have tested this out then and there. He should have tried making the motions of playing without producing the sound.

We have seen how the experimenter who beat on tin cans and blew bugles near a blindfolded cobra got no reaction at all. But when the blindfold was removed and the experimenter waved his arms, the cobra raised its head and followed the movements, just as it follows the movements of the Indian snake charmer. In the same way male snakes are attracted to female snakes by their movements.

Although snakes are deaf, they are sensitive to vibrations from the ground. If somebody walks near a snake, it faces the direction from which the vibrations come.

Since snakes do not hear each other, what does the rattle of the rattlesnake mean in its life? The best answer we have to this is that the rattle may warn away enemies. Fortunately it warns us too.

Smell plays a great role in the life of a snake. Snakes recognize each other by smell, and one snake can follow a trail made by another. If an artificial trail is made by rubbing the skin of one snake along a smooth surface, a second snake will follow it. Snakes follow such trails when they parade to their winter hibernating dens. A snake den contains many snakes, each one having followed the skin odors of the snake which went before it.

The Alligator's Voice

Four male alligators lived in a tank in the laboratory of

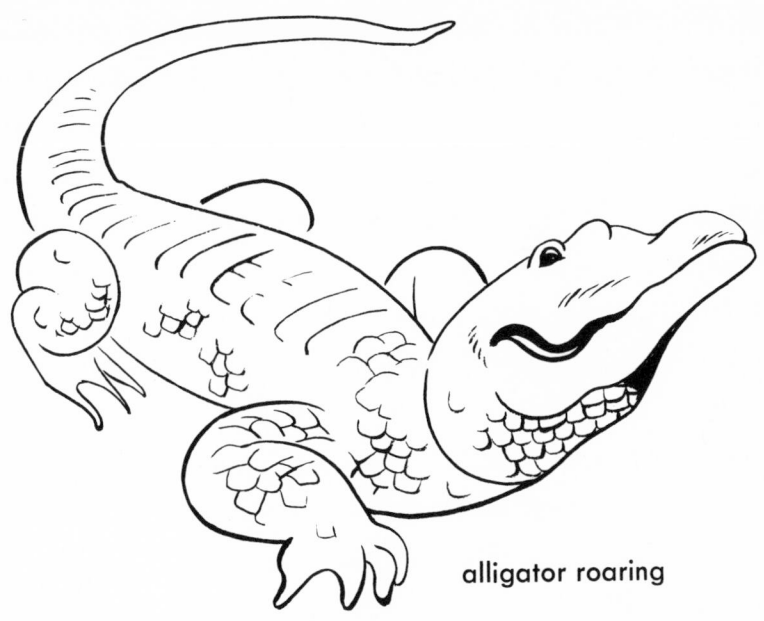

alligator roaring

the Animal Behavior Department of the American Museum of Natural History. Accidentally, it was discovered that when a slender steel rod near the tank was struck, the largest alligator roared. As a result, a series of experiments was started.

The largest alligator was put into a separate tank. First, the experiments discovered that the tone the steel rod gave when it was struck was a B flat, two octaves below middle C. This note was roughly the same pitch as the alligator's roar. Whether a French horn or a cello played this note, the alligator responded in the same way. He threw his head up, inflated his body with air, and then roared as he contracted his body and forced the air through his throat. He also moved toward the source of the sound and humped up his back.

When another male alligator was put into his tank, the big alligator roared at him and moved to attack him with his humped-up aggressive posture. Evidently the sight of another male alligator as well as the sound of one, produces bellowing and the start of an attack. All of this suggests that the male alligator roars to keep other male alligators out of his territory. Most roaring is done by alligators during the breeding season in early summer.

Female alligators lay their eggs in a big heap of decaying vegetation and then cover them with more decaying plant trash and some mud. When the little alligators are ready to hatch, they make a grunting sound, *umph, umph, umph.* This is a signal to the mother alligator, and she removes the top layer of debris from the eggs. The young ones then scramble out of the nest, and the mother leads the way to the water with a special low musical *umph* sound.

A mother alligator stays with her young for a short time, and during this period she warns them of danger with a special low grunt that sends all the young ones sliding off the banks into the water. The baby alligators also have their own special little distress grunt that brings the mother alligator to them.

CHAPTER 4

The Language of Birds

If all the eligible bachelors in a town should rent apartments with balconies and stand on them singing beautiful songs to attract the girls who pass by and to keep all rivals away, we would get some picture of what goes on in the bird world.

The male bird generally arrives first in the spring and claims a piece of ground. Then he picks a prominent place in a tree or bush and sings from this perch. Once headquarters are established, no other male can enter without a fight. The fight is usually only a singing contest that ends with the rival leaving occupied territory.

Suppose robin number one, who has already claimed a territory, hears a strange voice. It is that of a newcomer male robin who has entered the area and started to sing. Robin number one sings back loudly. The newcomer sings again.

Robin number one sings again, but this time nearer to the rival. Nearer and nearer he approaches, singing all the time, and being answered by the intruder. Finally robin number one gets close enough to robin number two to force him to take off, even though they may never actually see each other.

This is the way a male bird usually responds to the call of another male bird at breeding time in the spring. Scientists often take advantage of this habit. If they have only poor recordings of the song of a particular bird and want to improve them, they take tape recorder and loudspeaker into the field and play the bird's own song back to him. This usually brings the bird right down to the speaker where a good close recording of the song can be made. If a mirror is set up near the speaker, so that the bird can see himself, he will often fight his image in the mirror at the same time.

Woodpeckers cannot sing, but they too stake out a territory, prevent rivals from entering it if they can, and advertise their presence to the females. But they replace the voice with a loud drumming on hollow trees. Before a male black woodpecker finds a mate, he drums five to six hundred times a day. The sounds can be heard up to three quarters of a mile away, so males or females who enter the area can easily locate the drummer.

The female birds, who arrive after the males, have only

male bird staking a claim

woodpecker drumming

to respond to sound signals to locate a mate. When a female enters the territory of a male, she may be recognized by her looks, for often the female bird has much duller plumage than that of the male bird. In turn, the female bird may recognize the male by his looks. For example, a male flicker has a heavy black moustache on each side of the bill under the eyes. This is the sign of his "maleness." If you paint a black moustache on the face of a female flicker, and send her back

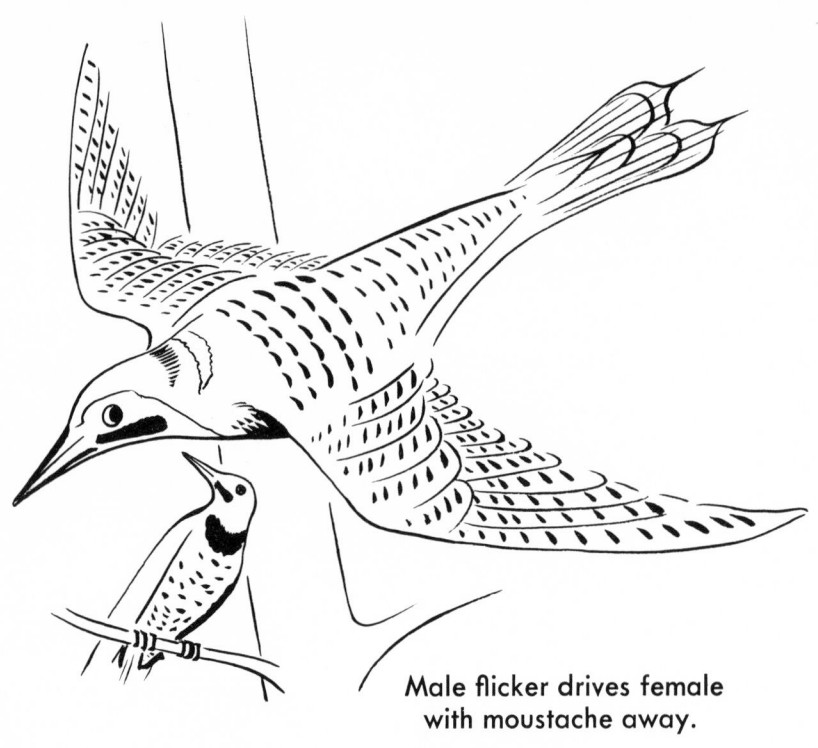

Male flicker drives female
with moustache away.

to her nesting hole, the male no longer recognizes her and drives her off.

But often looks alone are not enough, for in many species of birds the male and female look alike. Here sign language as well as sound comes into play.

A male and female song sparrow look alike. When they meet for the first time, the male bristles at the stranger. But the stranger does not fight or run away like a male. It just crouches and makes a soft, peculiar call. By this sign, the male recognizes a female song sparrow.

Some other female birds do the same thing; they simply stand firm instead of running away. But many other birds go through more elaborate routines.

Courtship Signals

Suppose we are watching a male black-headed gull stand

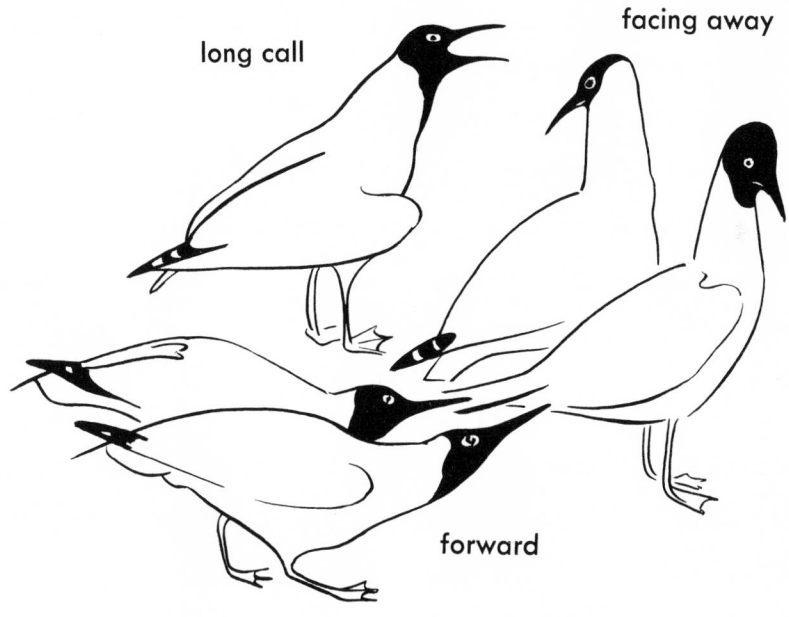

long call

facing away

forward

black-headed gulls

on his breeding grounds and give his "long call," which is a special mating call. Strange males avoid this gull, but unmated females are attracted. One alights near him. Then both gulls adopt a forward posture. A few seconds later, they change positions and adopt an upright posture with their heads turned away from each other. Then the female flies off. She visits a series of males and each time goes through the same set of postures. Sooner or later she becomes attached to one male, alights near him over and over again, and each time goes through the same performance—forward, upright with head facing away. Later the female does some "head tossing," and the male brings her food. If the two birds do not go through these movements, they do not mate.

Such strange movements and calls have become part of the recognition ceremonies of many birds in courtship. They may sing special songs, display their bright-colored plumage, strut around, make sudden flights into the air, bow, click bills, or offer bits of nesting material or food.

A male heron sits on a tree in his territory, points his beak to the sky, and calls *hoo,* after which he lowers his body into the nest and calls *ooo.* Hour after hour he calls for a partner. When a female bird arrives, he may drive her off at first, but in the end he offers her a stick. If she accepts it from him, they become a pair who mate and build a nest together.

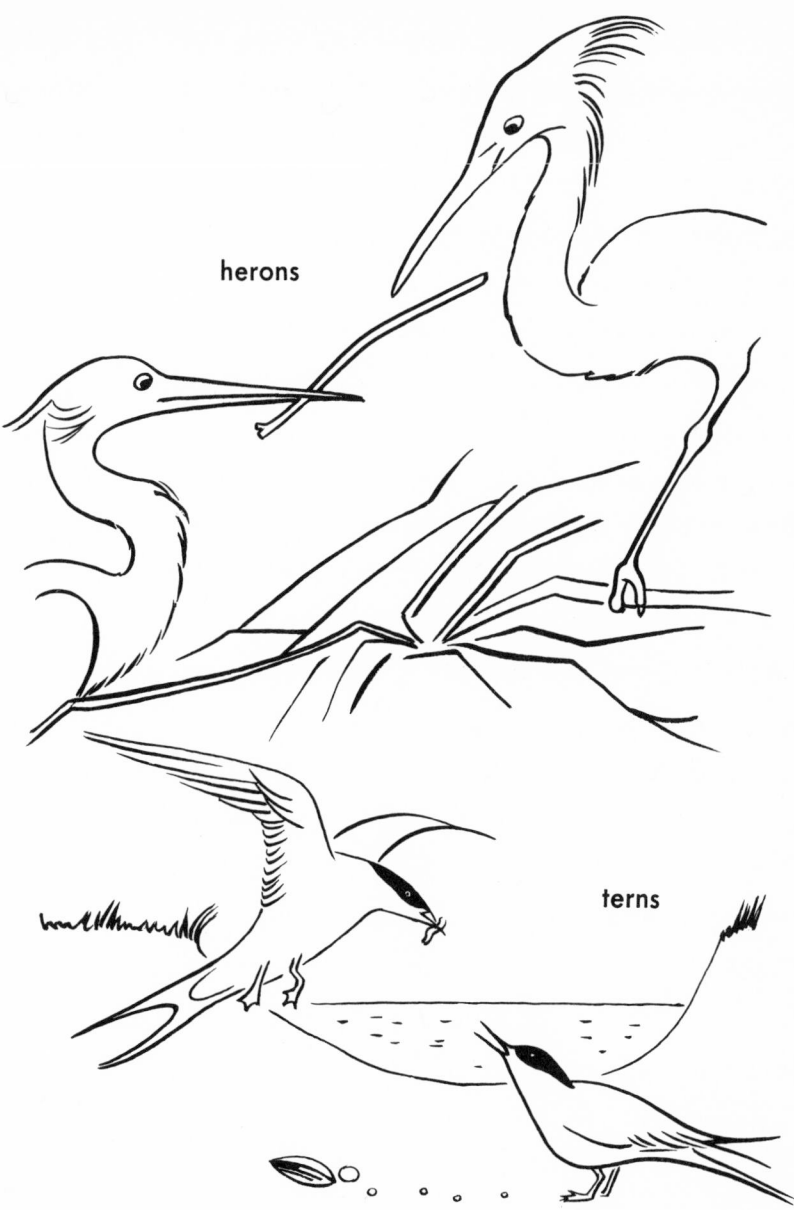

herons

terns

A male common tern catches a fish in his beak and parades up and down the beach with it until another tern comes up to him and accepts the fish. The female looks just like him, but by accepting the fish, she is recognized as a female. Often the male doesn't quite let go of the fish, and there is a little tug of war between them.

A male penguin waddles up to a female and places a gift of a pebble at her feet. If the gift is accepted, he has found a female.

A male peacock has a beautiful fan of iridescent gold and green feathers. This is his display material. When he meets a female he raises his gorgeous train, walks backward toward her, then suddenly turns around, clatters his quills together, stamps his feet, and lets out a piercing scream. In this ceremony the peacock, like many other birds, uses sight, sound, and movement all together.

In addition to songs that advertise territorial rights and invite females, and calls used in courtship ceremonies, there are many other kinds of call notes that have nothing to do with mating.

Mother-Young Signals

A long, careful study of the call notes of the chicken shows how important such signals are in the life of these birds. Within fifteen minutes after hatching, chicks give distress

penguin courtship

peacock displaying

Hen ignores
chick she
cannot hear.

calls if they are lost, cold, or hungry. A chick may be hidden
from the hen, but when it gives a distress call, the hen goes
in the direction of the sound. An experimenter once placed a
chick in a glass jar so no sound could be heard, although the
hen could see the chick clearly. Without the sound signal,
the hen took no notice of the chick.

The chicks are attracted to the mother hen by three different
vocal signals. When she walks along she keeps up a *clucking*
sound, and the chicks act as if the mother were saying "follow
me." When the hen discovers a source of food, she makes a
sound like *kuk-kuk-kuk-kuk* very rapidly, and her chicks

come running from all directions for food. At night she gives a roosting call — a long, low purr, which brings the chicks close to her.

The hen has a number of warning sounds, too, that control the behavior of her brood. When a hawk flies over the barnyard, the hen gives a raucous long drawn-out scream. The chicks at once run and hide under the nearest shelter. But when a dog intrudes into the barnyard, the hen gives a different warning — *cut-cut-cut-cut-kaaah!* If she is only moderately disturbed, she gives a low, brief, harsh alerting call, which makes the chicks stop and freeze to attention.

Using sound spectrograms (the pictures made by recorded sounds), scientists have found that there are some characteristics common to sounds that attract chicks. They are usually brief low notes repeated frequently. Even the sound of the tapping of a pencil on a table strongly attracts chicks. On the other hand, the warning sounds usually have long continuous higher notes. The scraping of a chair over a stone floor is very much like a warning scream and sends the chicks to cover.

Alarm Calls

Gulls have an amazing number of voice signals. Through autumn and winter they live in large flocks. Try to approach

spectogram pictures

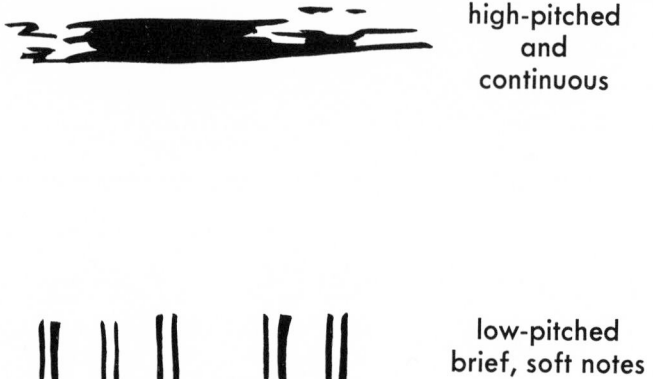

high-pitched
and
continuous

low-pitched
brief, soft notes

such a flock, and they will stop, crane their necks, and look at you. One of the gulls may suddenly give an attention call at which all the gulls rise and fly toward the source of the sound. Then a real alarm note may be sounded at which the gulls will circle higher and higher and fly away. These calls were recorded with a tape recorder and then broadcast to the gulls through loud-speakers. All the gulls at first approached the speakers, and then the whole flock left. The results of these experiments prompted a scientist to try this out at garbage dumps and fish-meal factories. The dump at one moment would be crowded with shrieking gulls, but when an alarm call was broadcast, all the gulls within the radius of half a mile rose into the air and circled away. Within a few minutes the place was deserted.

Even while still inside the egg, a gull chick stops squeaking when it hears an alarm call. A newly born gull chick reacts to this sound by crouching in the nest. Before it is a day old, it will leave the nest during the alarm and crouch some distance away in the sand. The brownish-gray color of a chick becomes almost invisible against the background of the sand. Every day the chicks move farther and farther away, until each one has its own special hiding place to go to when the alarm is sounded.

The practical method of scaring gulls away with their own alarm calls has been used on starlings too. When a starling is held in the hand, it shrieks loudly. This distress call was recorded to see if it would keep starlings away from a town where they had become great pests, roosting by the thousands on its buildings and trees. At sunset, as the birds came in to roost, a sound truck played back the recording of the distress call. The starlings left. For five successive nights, as the starlings started to fly in, the sound truck went into action. After the fifth night the starlings stayed away.

Food Calls

If you have ever been on a fishing boat at sea, you must

starlings coming in to roost

have heard another cry of the gulls, the food call. A gull may be flying alone behind the boat, but if you throw a fish to him, other gulls soon gather. They are attracted by a three-note call. When this food call was recorded and played back to the gulls, they came soaring in from as far as two to three miles away, even from around points of land hidden from sight.

A parent gull gives a *mew* call, and this makes a baby gull beg for food by pecking at the parent gull's bill. A sight signal is important here too. The bill tip of the herring gull

sea gulls gathering

has a red color patch that stands out against the yellow background of the bill. Experiments with stuffed painted head models showed that the red patch is a sight signal that makes the young gull peck for food.

Young robins, while their eyes are still closed, open their big mouths in response to any movement of the nest. The young mouths are always open ready to receive food, when their parents land on the nest, jarring it slightly. A week later, when the robins can see, they open their mouths only when they see the parents or hear them give a low, whistling

Baby gull pecks at
red spot on mother's bill.

feeding note. Then they in turn give a food-begging call. Much later, when they have left the nest, this same hunger call helps the parents locate the young ones.

Group Signals

Flocks of songbirds communicate by calls all the time. Twenty such small birds may be feeding on the ground when one of them flies up into a low bush and calls. As it calls, it

mobbing

taking cover

hops higher in the bush. Some of the birds on the ground stop feeding, and also hop into the bushes making the same calling sounds. After a few seconds one bird flies off and one or two others follow. They keep flying from bush to bush, calling. One by one the remaining birds stop feeding and hop up, till all move off through the bushes. In this way, the flock keeps together as it drifts through the trees.

When a hawk flies over, the first bird to see it gives a high-pitched squeaky sound and flies to cover. All the other birds do likewise. But if one of the birds sees a hawk sitting in a tree, it gives a *tsip* or *twink* or *chink* call, which calls attention to the predator. The whole crowd of birds then mob the hawk, flying around it with a chorus of cries.

We have to remember that birds do not make these sounds with the idea of communicating with other birds. They make them even when no other birds are around to hear them. But if other birds are present, they respond to these signals. Many of the signals play an important role in a bird's life. As we have seen, they may help birds find food, protect them from enemies, and make it possible for them to find a mate. Without such signals many birds would not be able to survive.

CHAPTER 5

Communication Between Mammals

Dogs, cats, rabbits, wolves, cows, deer, seals, monkeys, and apes are examples of mammals — warm-blooded animals with fur or hair that bear their young alive and feed them with milk from special mammary glands. What is their world like? And how do such animals communicate with each other? We hear many stories about mammals, and most of them make the animals seem almost human. It is hard for us to realize that they do not hear what we hear, see what we see, or feel what we feel. Only careful observations and experiments can open the window into their special world. A few scientists have spent years watching different groups of mammals, and from their patient work we have learned the little we know about these animals.

We don't expect a mammal to behave like a bird or a snake, because it has different sense organs, and hears, sees, and smells the world differently. Most mammals do not see colors, but see their surroundings in shades of gray. They have wonderful perception of movement. The slightest change in the position of a leg, tail, or head is quickly noticed. Most mammals have excellent hearing, and many communicate with each other by means of barks, howls, bleats, mews, snorts, and purrs. The sense of smell plays a big role in their lives. When a deer in a zoo is put into an area with another deer, the first thing it does is sniff the scent marks left by the other deer on twigs, branches, tree stumps, and stones.

The Dog's World

The dog's world is dominated by his sharp sense of smell. Experiments have shown that German police dogs can easily follow the trail of a horse or another dog. They can pick out this trail even though it is mixed up in a crisscrossing network of false tracks. In another experiment, a dog picked out the scent of one particular person on a handkerchief, and distinguished it from that of seven other people. The dog's landscape is more of a "smellscape" than a "seescape." You can see for yourself how a dog picks up smell signals of other dogs from every lamppost on the street, or from the stones and tree stumps it passes on a trail in the woods. A male dog recognizes a female dog by her scent. A little scent of a female

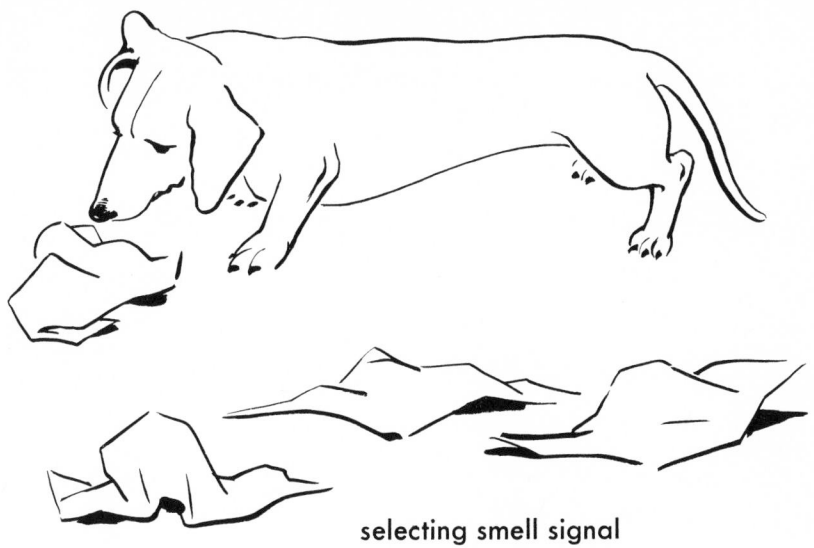

selecting smell signal

dog rubbed on a person's clothes will protect him from attacks by fierce male watchdogs. Burglars have been known to make use of this information.

Dogs communicate by sound, too, with whines, growls, and yips. We know from experiments that dogs hear very well. They can hear a sound four times farther away than we can. They also hear much higher notes than our ears can detect. There is a whistle called a Silent Dog Whistle, because its high tones are silent to us but can be heard by a dog. You can train a dog to come to you when you blow this whistle that your neighbors cannot hear.

Wolf and Fox Signals

The dog's cousins are wolves. The region they inhabit is full of sniffing posts at which smell signals are picked up. But sound signals are important to wolves too. Several wolves get together and howl before leaving on a hunt. This may serve as an assembly call. While the hunt is on, short, rapid barks keep them together, and deep snarls signal the closing in for the kill. A mother wolf's whine is a warning sound to her young and sends them scattering. One recent study shows how important sight signals are too. The picture shows the

wolves howling before hunt

normal timid

threatening suspicious

facial expressions of wolf

facial expressions of wolves. Notice how the positions of ears, mouth, eyes, and tail change with changing moods.

Red foxes have some of the same facial expressions. In anger, a fox, like a wolf, bares his teeth, and his neck hairs rise. When two male foxes fight, they stand on their hind legs, put their forepaws on each other's shoulders, and try to push each other down, screaming at one another all the while. A defeated fox walks away with his tail between his legs and his head down. When male and female foxes fight, the pattern is different. Both foxes sit on the ground facing each

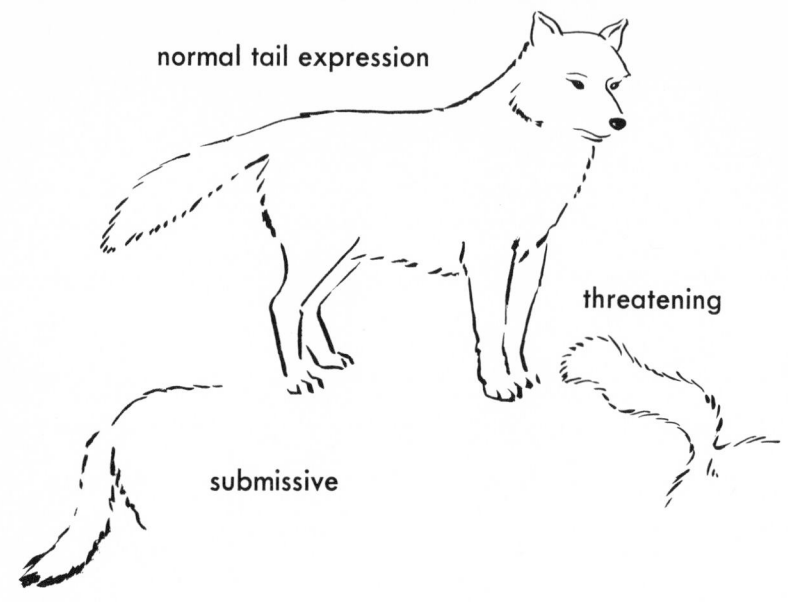

normal tail expression

threatening

submissive

other and scream. They may keep this up for fifteen minutes, although the cries grow softer as time goes on. It is a battle with voice only.

Rabbits, Opossums, and Squirrels

Warning sounds, calls from mother to young, calls from male to female, and calls that keep a group in contact, are used by many different mammals. When little rabbits cry *qua-a-a-a,* the mother rabbit comes running and chases the animal disturbing her nest. Mother opossums rush back to the den when baby opossums cry. If she gives them a clicking signal, they jump into her pouch or cling to her fur, and leave the den with her. If she doesn't click, they remain in the den. The California ground squirrel has three different kinds of warning calls, one for hawks, one for snakes, and one for dogs or people. The cry for a hawk sounds like *cheesk*. Other squirrels repeat the cry, and all rush to hide. When the enemy is a snake, the ground squirrel moves within a few feet of it, flicks its tail, and gives a peculiar chirp that sounds like *cheet-ik-irr-irr-irr*. Once scientists recognized this peculiar call, they were able to locate all the rattlesnakes in an area by following this cry. When a man or a dog gets too close to the ground squirrel it chirps *chwee-chu-chuk*.

The Prairie Dog

When animals live together in groups, they often have many signals that unite them. The prairie dog (really a ground squirrel) lives in "towns" dotted by mounds of soil. Each mound has a burrow entrance. At the approach of danger, one prairie dog may give a warning bark. Immediately all the other prairie dogs of the town sit up. If the bark becomes high-pitched and rapid, they stop whatever they are doing and dash into their burrows. Another type of call is the territorial call. The animal throws itself into an upright position and gives a loud, clear, two-syllable call. It usually means

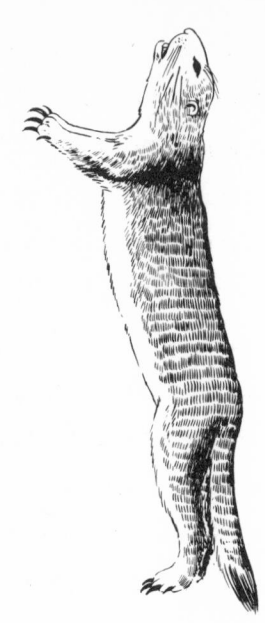

territorial call of prairie dog

"this is my territory — keep out," but sometimes it is used as an all-clear signal after danger is past, and then it is echoed by all the other prairie dogs in the town.

Deer Language

Signals of voice or gesture keep herds of deer co-ordinated. One of the larger members of the deer family is the American elk. The young are born in May and June, and groups of mother elk with their young stay together in nursery herds. There is a constant calling back and forth between calf and

nursery herd of elk

mother elk. A mature female is always the leader of such a nursery group. A motion of her head and neck can make the whole group turn in a different direction. When she gives the warning signal, a short snort, the whole herd takes flight immediately.

One scientist spent two years living with red deer in Scotland. He reports a different reaction to a warning signal. At the approach of danger, the lead cow gives a warning bark. But the rest do not immediately dash off. Instead, they fix their eyes on the cause of the disturbance, and then move off

mule deer

in quiet, orderly retreat while the enemy is kept in sight. The same kind of grunts and calls between calf and mother keep the two in contact, just as they do among elks.

Mule deer, with their big ears, are well known in the western part of North America. Careful studies show that these deer too have sound signals. An explosive snort warns other deer; bleating sounds exchanged between mother and fawns help keep them together. Under attack, a young fawn lets out a shrill, piercing scream that brings the mother doe to its defense. Several movements act as signals. When a mule

American pronghorn antelope

deer raises its head and cups its ears forward, it communicates an attention signal. If it suddenly bounds away, landing heavily on all four feet, it makes a crashing sound that serves as a warning message to other mule deer.

The American pronghorn antelope has a silent flashing signal. Its rump hairs are long and white. If the animal is disturbed or frightened, they are raised suddenly, and the white hairs flash in the light. A whole thundering herd of pronghorns will flee at this signal.

When other kinds of deer and antelope are studied, other

Alaska fur seals

kinds of defense signals may be found. These social animals that live in herds for part of the year and are easy prey to wildcats, wolves, and other meat-eating animals, are almost certain to have such means of communicating warning and danger signals. Otherwise, they would not have survived through the millions of years of their history on earth.

Alaska Fur Seals

When hundreds of thousands of animals congregate, even for a short time, communication signals play an important role in their life. Alaska fur seals gather every summer on the Pribilof Islands in the Bering Sea between Alaska and Siberia. Hundreds of thousands of females waddle out of the water onto the rocky and sandy shores of these islands and bear their young. The mother fur seal nurses no pup but her own. After about a week on land, she returns to the sea to feed, and comes back once a week to nurse her pup. But how can she find her own among the thousands on the beach?

Scientists observing these animals marked them so they could tell one from another. Then they found out that a particular mother always returns to the same part of the island she left. The pup meanwhile stays close to this area. When the mother seal comes ashore, she bleats like a sheep. Any hungry pups in the area bleat back and move toward her with their noses pointing forward. The mother seal sniffs at the nose of each pup, and in this way locates her own. Sound and smell signals are necessary to keep the new generation alive.

Monkeys and Apes

Monkeys and apes are the highest type of mammals next to man. They frequently travel in groups and take care of their young for a long time. What are their signal codes like?

howling monkeys

In the deep forests of Central and South America, howling monkeys live in clans. C. R. Carpenter, a biologist, spent about two years watching these monkeys and their ways. Through his work, we have learned how vocal signals operate to keep the clan together, to protect it from enemies, and to co-ordinate its activities.

Every morning and evening the forest echoes with the roars and howls of the howling monkeys. Each clan starts and ends the day by letting the neighboring clans know its position. Every clan has its own separate territory, but the territories overlap a bit. When one clan gets too close to another, there is a tremendous roaring on both sides until one or the other group moves off. Any alarming situation will bring forth this roaring, which prepares the whole group for attack or defense. If the situation is only mildly alarming, you hear a series of gurgling grunts. A grunt that sounds like *who who who* goes with strange situations and makes other members of the clan quiet and attentive.

Another signal keeps the clan together as it moves through the forest feeding on fruits, buds, and leaves. When the members of the clan have eaten their fill in one tree and are about to move on, all the males look for good tree routes (if there happen to be many possible ones). When any one of them finds an easy pathway through the trees, he gives a deep metallic cluck, and this makes the whole clan move toward him to follow his particular trail. Every once in a while, a young baby falls to the ground. The mother wails, and the baby cries in a high-pitched voice, so that the clan gets its location even though it may not be visible. Either the mother or a male member of the clan will then swoop down to the ground and pick up the baby in its arms. When the infant is in contact with its mother's body, it purrs.

As the baby howlers grow, they begin to play with one another. They make little chirping noises, and this seems to attract other young ones to join in the play. If the playing gets rough, an old male may suddenly grunt, and the young monkeys act as though somebody said, "Stop that noise," for they either stop or play more quietly.

The language of howlers is limited, but it serves to unify their activities in the jungle where overhanging leaves often hide them from one another.

Carpenter also studied the apes called gibbons in their natural home in the forests of Thailand. He found that they too have calls that proclaim territory and alarm, calls that direct the movements of a group through the trees, and calls that bring the males of the family swinging to lost baby gibbons.

Chimpanzees are the smartest of the apes. There have not been many studies of them in their native home in equatorial Africa, but we know a lot about them because they live well

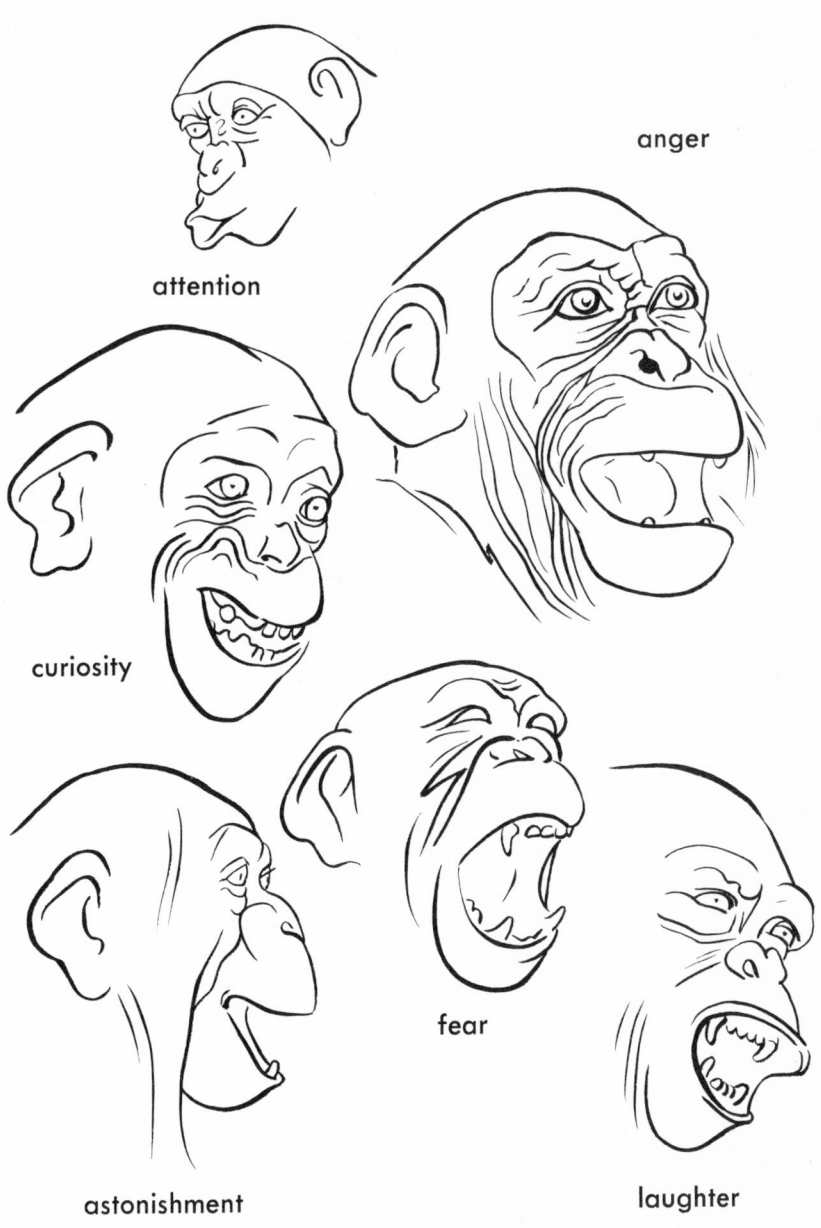

attention

anger

curiosity

astonishment

fear

laughter

facial expressions of chimpanzee

in captivity. A chimpanzee can't talk, but it communicates with its whole body and face, and with grunts, cries, screams, whimpers, chatters, and shouts. If a chimpanzee is excited, he jumps up and down. If he is disappointed, he swings and waves his arms above his head. In despair, he throws himself upon the floor on his back and rolls wildly from side to side. If he wants something, he shows what by his actions. He pulls on another chimp and imitates walking to get him to accompany him. If he wants to be scratched, he puts out a hand to someone who might scratch him, and scratches himself with his other hand.

A chimpanzee's face is full of expression. The picture shows it ruled by different emotions.

Thirty-two different kinds of sounds have been recorded for chimpanzees. Short *ho ho ho* sounds are warning sounds. *Ooh ooh ooh* sounds express fear. A *gahk* sound is connected with food. A chimpanzee communicates with other members of his social group constantly.

And so we see that all kinds of mammals have a language. It is not a language in the human sense, for they do not communicate with words and sentences. But they do have signals, most of which have to do with food, enemies, mother-young ties, meeting of the sexes, or keeping the members of a group in touch with each other.

CHAPTER 6

Insect Signal Codes

As we have seen, secret worlds of communication among animals are difficult to penetrate. But sometimes the brilliant work of one scientist can reveal truths that are almost more fantastic than fiction. Professor Karl von Frisch has thrown great light on the remarkable ways honeybees communicate in their dark hives. The series of experiments he did with these insects are models of work done by scientific method and wonderful examples of the clear, logical thinking that is so much a part of every good scientific experiment.

Von Frisch had worked with bees for many years. He was puzzled by something he had observed repeatedly. When he set up a table, on which he placed little dishes of scented honey, he attracted bees. Usually he had to wait for hours or days until a bee discovered the feeding place. But as soon as one bee discovered it, many more came to it in a short

observation hive

time. Evidently the one bee was able to communicate the news of food to other bees in its hive.

How was this possible? To find out, von Frisch constructed special hives, containing only one honeycomb, that had a glass wall through which he could watch what went on inside. He also wanted to identify the bees, so he painted them with little spots of color, which enabled him to tell them apart.

When a marked bee returned to the hive from the feeding table, von Frisch watched through the glass. To his amazement, the bee began to perform a dance on the vertical surface

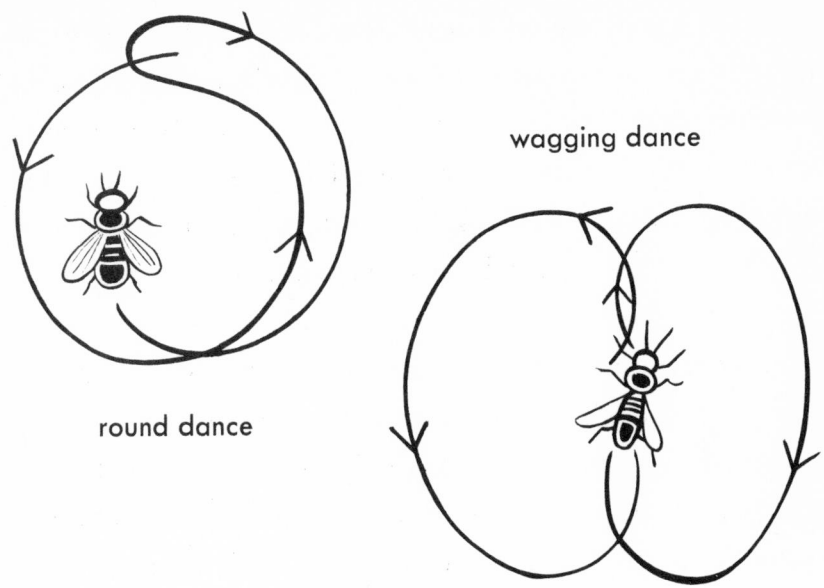

wagging dance

round dance

of the honeycomb. First she made a circle to the right, then to the left, and she repeated these circles over and over.

But that was not all. The dance seemed to excite the surrounding bees. They trooped behind the first dancer, as she circled, and imitated her movements. Then the bees left the hive and went to the feeding place. Evidently the circle dance communicated news of food. But what else did it tell? Did it tell in what direction the food was?

Von Frisch's next experiment set out to answer this question. At four points around the hive, ten yards to the north, east, south, and west, he set down a glass dish with sugar water scented with honey. Several marked bees then were fed at the west point. In a short time he had his answer. Bees came to all the dishes regardless of the direction. The circle dance told the bees to fly out and seek food in the immediate neighborhood of the hive, but it did not communicate any information about direction.

After many experiments, von Frisch began to suspect that the dancing might reveal the distance the bees had to cover to find the feeding place. He tested this idea with the following experiment. He set up two feeding places—one a few yards from the hive and the other 300 yards from the hive. He marked all the bees that came to the nearby feeding station blue and all the bees that went to the faraway station red. When the bees came back to the observation hive, von Frisch saw a curious sight. All the bees that had been marked blue at the nearby feeding station were doing the circling dance. All the bees that were marked red at the distant station were doing an entirely different kind of dance, a wagging dance. The dancer ran a short distance in a straight line up the honeycomb wagging her abdomen very rapidly from side to side. Then she turned in a semicircle, ran straight ahead again, turned in another semicircle to the opposite side, and continued to repeat the pattern over and over. It was clear now.

The circle dance meant food was near. The wagging dance meant food was far away.

But then another question arose. Did the wagging dance tell the bees how far away food was? To answer this, von Frisch and his co-workers set up a feeding site 100 yards from the hive and then moved it gradually farther away, up to a distance of 10,000 yards. Back at the hive they watched the wagging dance closely. With a stop watch they counted the number of times the whole dance was repeated per minute. The dance was repeated very quickly—about 10 times every 15 seconds—when the distance between the hive and the feeding place was 100 yards. At 1000 yards the dance was re-peated about 5 times every 15 seconds. At 10,000 yards the dance was only carried through once every 15 seconds. The farther the distance, the slower was the dance. So another amazing fact came to light. The number of times per minute the wagging dance was done told the bees in the hive the distance to the feeding place.

This conclusion was not lightly arrived at. The scientists observed 3885 dances in the course of this experiment. Von Frisch himself wondered, "Can they really do this?" He set up more experiments to find out how accurately the distance could be judged. The bees always came to the feeding place at the correct distance.

Von Frisch thought then that it would be of little use to the bees to know the distance to a faraway feeding place, or to certain flowers blooming a long distance from the hive, if they did not know their direction. He set out to discover whether the wagging dance indicated direction.

He repeated the experiment he had done with the circle dance, but this time the feeding place was over 200 yards

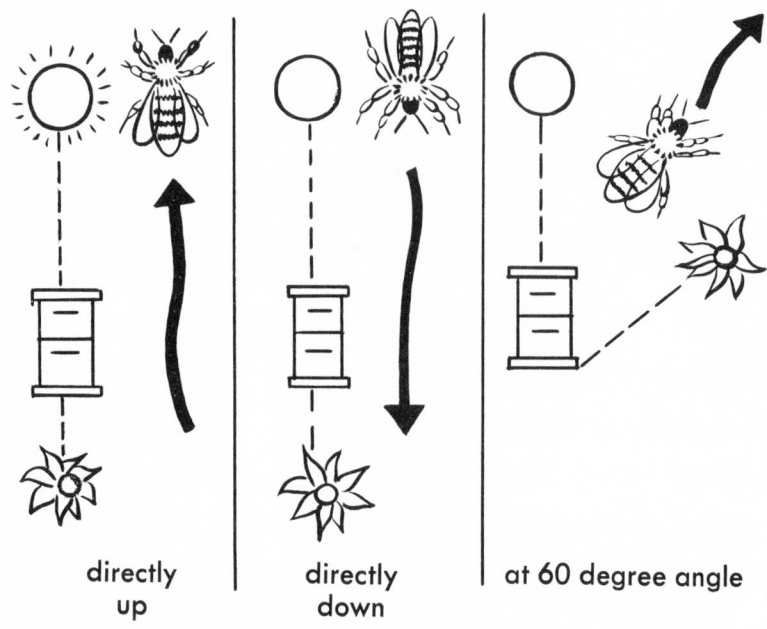

directly	directly	at 60 degree angle
up	down	

Direction of straight
part of wagging dance indicates
direction of food.

away. The results were exciting. The bees did not fly out in all directions. If the feeding place was 200 yards to the west, they came there. If it was shifted to 200 yards to the east, they went to the east.

When the scientists watched the dances for a long time, while the sugar was always at the same feeding place, they noticed that the direction of the straight part of the wagging dance gradually shifted. It was different in the morning from what it was in the afternoon. To von Frisch it became clear that the straight part of the dance was shifting with the sun's position. He came to the conclusion that the bee dance must signal direction in relation to the position of the sun in the sky.

If a dancer headed directly upward during the straight part of her wagging dance, the feeding place was toward the sun. If the straight run pointed downward, the feeding place was away from the sun. If the straight part of the dance was sixty degrees to the left of vertical, the feeding place was sixty degrees to the left of the sun, and so on. They found the wagging dance of the honeybee was a remarkable indicator of the direction of food.

Von Frisch later found that bees see the light of the sky differently from the way we do. Through their eyes the light is polarized, just as it is through a Polaroid filter. Such a

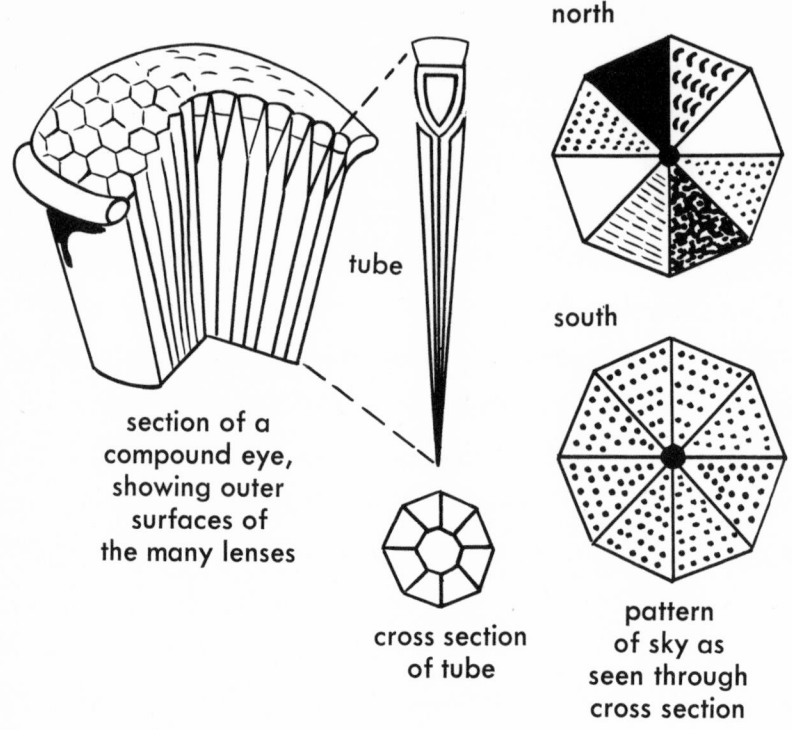

north

tube

south

section of a
compound eye,
showing outer
surfaces of
the many lenses

cross section
of tube

pattern
of sky as
seen through
cross section

filter allows rays to travel in only one direction instead of being scattered in all directions. The bee's eyes are compound, that is, made up of many small eyes set together, and they act like a mosaic of Polaroid filters. We may see the sky as all blue, but the bees see a different pattern of light in the sky for each direction of the compass. The pattern in these different directions depends on the position of the sun.

How should the results of von Frisch's experiments be interpreted? Do they show that bees are intelligent, and have minds that figure out directions and distances? There is no scientific reason to say so. It is much more likely that during the millions of years honeybees have lived on the earth, they gradually developed this inborn, complicated pattern of communication. Von Frisch himself thought it would be interesting to "investigate more primitive social insects to learn whether they have a simpler kind of language which would show us how the complex situation in the honeybee may have developed."

There is more to the story of honeybee communication. Recently biologists in England observed a remarkable sharing of food among bees in a colony. They fed six bees from a colony of about 25,000 with sugar syrup containing radioactive phosphorus. Even the tiniest amount of this substance can be detected in a bee's body because of its radioactivity. The six bees returned to the hive. In four hours almost one fifth of all the bees in the hive were radioactive! In a few days most of the bees in the hive were radioactive. They thus learned that when bees are collecting a certain kind of nectar they will quickly share it among the members of the colony.

Another biologist found that worker bees lick a substance from the body of the queen bee and pass it from bee to bee in the food they share. Even though the thousands of bees in a colony cannot possibly see the queen, they are aware of her presence by this secretion from her body. If the queen bee is removed, the workers in the hive become aware of her absence in an hour or two and start to search for her. If the "queen bee substance" gets low, the workers start to rear another queen.

And so the world of the honeybee is just beginning to be opened to us. We have found out more about what really goes on inside the hive, but we haven't learned that the honeybee is clever or intelligent.

The Ant World

The ant world has always kept scientists wondering. What means of communication do ants use? Many ants see only dimly, but are very sensitive to odors. They do not have noses like ours but smell with their feelers, or antennae. Watch two ants meet each other, and see how they stop and tap one another with their antennae. They are exchanging smell signals, and in this way recognize members of their own colony. When an ant leaves the nest or comes back to it, it touches the ground every once in a while with the tip of its abdomen and deposits a bit of scent. A series of these spots blazes a trail for the ants that follow. That is why you soon find many ants in your kitchen after one ant has discovered a bit of sweet food left

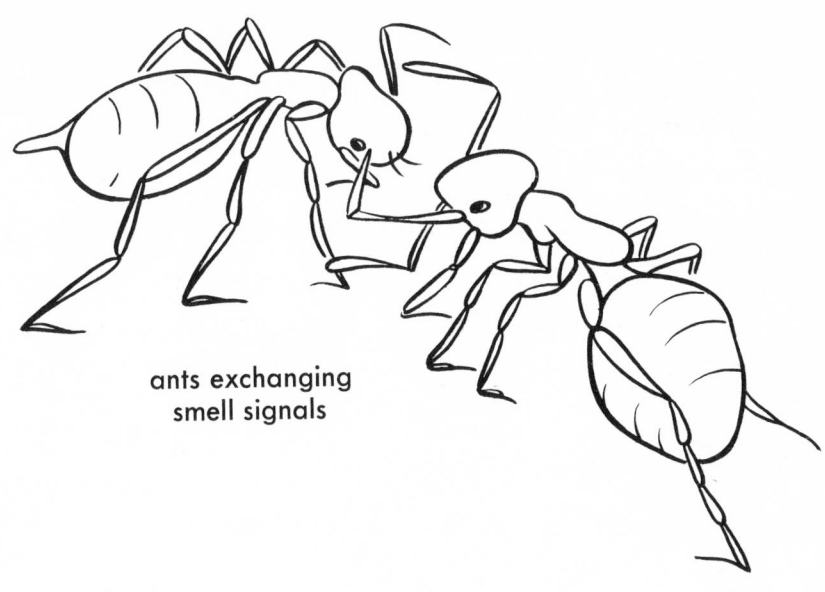

ants exchanging
smell signals

open there. If you happen to be watching such a line of ants moving toward food, just rub your finger across their path. You will see the way they react to your breaking of their chemical trail.

An ant that has found food goes back to the ant colony and dashes around. This excites other ants in the colony, who then run out and follow the chemical track laid down by the first ant. Some scientists think that the key to the ant world is in their sensitivity to the slightest movement of other ants. Experiments have shown that some ants learn more quickly than others, are more excitable, and are also the ones in the colony that tend to start off all the different jobs, such as nest building and searching for food. The other ants near these excitement-center ants start to do the same jobs, because they are aroused by the movements of their neighbors. So all the complicated work in an ant colony gets done because ants are so sensitive to their fellow ants and copy their movements.

Moth Signals

While ants "keep their noses (antennae) to the ground"

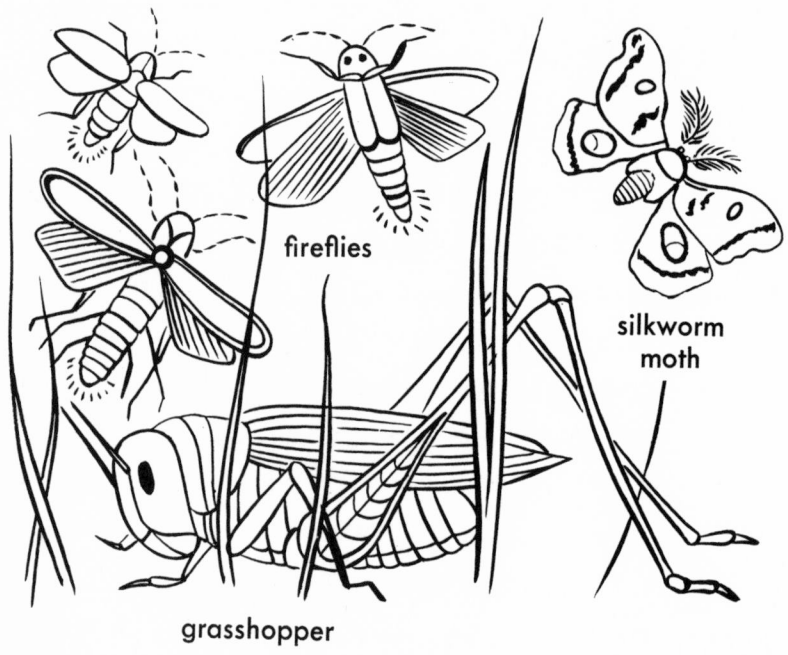

fireflies

silkworm moth

grasshopper

when following smell signals, moths follow such signals through the air for great distances. Long ago, in 1895, a scientist kept a female silkworm moth in a small wicker cage outdoors, and then released a male silkworm moth a mile and a half away. The male was marked with a silk thread so that he could be identified. The next morning the marked male was at the cage of the female.

How could such a faint smell travel for such a distance? We cannot smell it even when we hold the moth up to our nose. Yet the smell organs of the moth on its antennae can pick up this faraway signal. The mystery was solved when it was discovered that male moths can only locate females far away when the wind is blowing. When the wind brings the tiny scent particles from the female moth, the male moth heads straight into the wind that carries the scent. He zigzags toward the female until the scent is so strong that he can fly directly to her.

Light Signals of the Firefly

Male and female fireflies attract each other with light signals. There may be many different kinds of fireflies flitting around in the dark of night, yet each kind has its own particular way of flashing. Some have long flashes, others have short ones; some go on and off, others stay lit steadily; some have a special rhythm.

One kind of firefly flashes exactly once every 5.8 seconds! The female must flash back exactly two seconds afterward in order to be recognized by the male. Experiments showed that this firefly would approach any light as long as it flashed back exactly two seconds after he did.

Sound Signals

Insects communicate with sound signals too. As long ago as 1878, an electric lighting system was being set up in New York, and one of the dynamos gave off a buzzing sound. All the male mosquitoes in the neighborhood gathered around the dynamo. Recent experiments have shown that the hateful whine we hear when a female mosquito approaches us sounds like a love call to a male mosquito. The sound is made by the beating of her wings in flight. Imitate the same sound with an electrical apparatus and the males will gather around the machine, as they did around the dynamo. Male mosquitoes have been trapped this way. If the males are caught before they mate, these sound traps can reduce the mosquito population greatly. So far, however, no large-scale practical tests have been tried.

All through the summer we hear grasshoppers, katydids, crickets, and cicadas rasping out their songs by rubbing one part of their bodies against another part. Sometimes two wings are rubbed together. Sometimes a leg is rubbed against a wing. Occasionally, there is a special sound-producing organ. But it all results in the buzzings, creakings, scrapings, and rattlings we are familiar with. Day and night the choruses go on. Some of the insects sing only when the first rays of the sun filter through the trees at dawn. Others start when the sun is bright. Still other choruses break out when the light fails at dusk. Then when these stop, the night-singing choruses begin. Are the insects communicating with each other?

Recent work has shown that usually the males do the singing, and these sounds serve as calling sounds to the females. The females, attracted by the calls, move toward the males until they are close enough to mate. This has been proved by experiments with tape-recorded male calling sounds. When these are played back to the females of the same kind, the females move toward the mechanical sound just as they move toward the calling male.

Imagine the grasses, trees, and bushes alive with thousands of insects. In this great crowd, a female snowy tree cricket has to find a male snowy tree cricket. A female bush katydid has to find a male of exactly her kind. It all seems quite possible when you find out that every kind of cricket, katydid, grasshopper, or cicada has its own particular beat and rhythm that only its own females will answer to.

The calling song sometimes collects other males too. You can find crowds of male cicadas piled on top of one another and singing away together. Females are attracted to these dense colonies of males.

In a few cases, the females have an answering song, and the males move toward the females. A male grasshopper, sitting in the grass, may signal. If a female answers, the male starts toward her, although she may be hidden from sight. In about four seconds, he signals again. If the female answers, he moves on through the grass, keeping his bearing for another four seconds. He has to keep giving the signals and hearing the return song every four seconds in order to reach the female. This is true of one kind of grasshopper. Others may alternate signals at different time intervals, and in some cases both the males and females move toward each other.

The steady insect hum of summertime is not a mere noise, but a signal code that plays an important role in the life of the insects.

If you happen to have close contact with a special kind of animal, and want to learn more about animal communication, start a reading program using the bibliography that follows. It will help prepare you to do your own experiments. Amateurs have contributed a great deal to our knowledge of this subject. If you are a keen observer, you may too. You will also find many surprises in the animal world.

Bibliography

(P) means paperback

Armstrong, Edward A. *The Way Birds Live.* Lindsay Drummond Ltd., 1943.

Bell, P. R. *Darwin's Biological Work, Some Aspects Reconsidered.* Cambridge University Press, 1959.

Bonner, J. T. *Cells and Societies.* Princeton University Press, 1955.

Bourliere, F. *The Natural History of Mammals.* A. A. Knopf, 1954.

Burns, Eugene. *The Sex Life of Wild Animals.* Premier Books, 1956. (P)

Buddenbrock, Wolfgang von. *The Senses.* University of Michigan Press, 1958.

Carthy, J. D. *The World of Feeling.* Roy Publishers, 1960.

Crompton, John. *Ways of the Ant.* Houghton Mifflin, 1954.

Fox, H. Munro. *Personality of Animals,* rev. ed. Penguin Books, 1952. (P)

Frisch, Karl von. *Bees, Their Vision, Chemical Senses, and Language.* Cornell University Press, 1950.

The Dancing Bees. Harcourt Brace, 1955.

Goetsch, Wilhelm. *The Ants.* University of Michigan Press, 1957. (P)

Hediger, H. *Wild Animals in Captivity.* Academic Press, 1950.

Heinroth, Oskar and Katharana. *The Birds.* University of Michigan Press, 1958. (P)

Howard, H. E. *Territory in Bird Life.* Murray, Ltd., 1920.

Lack, D. *The Life of the Robin.* Penguin Books, 1943. (P)

Lanyon, W. E. and Tavolga, W. N. *Animal Sounds and Communication.* American Institute of Biological Sciences, 1960.

Lorenz, Konrad Z. *King Solomon's Ring.* Thomas Y. Crowell Co., 1952.

Morley, Derek W. *The Ant World.* Penguin Books, 1953. (P)

Noble, Ruth C. *Nature of the Beast.* Doubleday, 1945.

Scott, J. P. *Animal Behavior.* University of Chicago Press, 1958.

Seton, Ernest T. *Lives of the Game Animals.* Doubleday, 1929.

Tinbergen, Niko. *The Herring Gull's World.* Frederick Praeger, 1953.

   The Herring Gull's World, rev. ed. Basic Books, 1961.

Most of these books have bibliographies too, so you can go on and on. The best bibliography of scientific papers published on the subject of animal communication is in *Animal Sounds and Communication,* edited by W. E. Lanyon and W. N. Tavolga. It comes with a record to illustrate many of the points discussed in in the book.

Magazines like *Scientific American, Natural History,* and *Audubon Magazine* often have articles on animal communication.

INDEX

95